EXPLORING WORLD CULTURES

Spain

Joanne Mattern

Cavendish
Square

New York

Published in 2017 by Cavendish Square Publishing, LLC
243 5th Avenue, Suite 136, New York, NY 10016

Library of Congress Cataloging-in-Publication Data

Names: Mattern, Joanne, 1963- author.
Title: Spain / Joanne Mattern.
Description: New York : Cavendish Square Publishing, [2017] | Series: Exploring world cultures | Includes index.
Identifiers: LCCN 2016027440 (print) | LCCN 2016027991 (ebook) | ISBN 9781502621467 (pbk.) | ISBN 9781502621474 (6 pack) | ISBN 9781502621481 (library bound) | ISBN 9781502621498 (ebook)
Subjects: LCSH: Spain--Juvenile literature.
Classification: LCC DP17 .M375 2017 (print) | LCC DP17 (ebook) | DDC 946--dc23
LC record available at https://lccn.loc.gov/2016027440

Editorial Director: David McNamara
Editor: Kristen Susienka
Copy Editor: Rebecca Rohan
Associate Art Director: Amy Greenan
Designer: Joseph Macri
Production Coordinator: Karol Szymczuk
Photo Research: J8 Media

The photographs in this book are used by permission and through the courtesy of: Cover Maria Teijeiro/Digital Vision/Getty Images; p. 5 Anton_Ivanov/Shutterstock.com; p. 6 Rainer Lesniewski/Shutterstock.com; p. 7 Sloot/iStock/Thinkstock; p. 8 Ivy Close Images/Alamy Stock Photo; p. 9 Time Life Pictures/Pictures Inc./The LIFE Picture Collection/Getty Images; p. 10 Chema Moya/AFP/Getty Images; p. 11 Jorisvo/Shutterstock.com; p. 12 Alberto Loyo/Shutterstock.com; p. 14 Salparadis/Shutterstock.com; p. 15 Paul Preece/Alamy Stock Photo; p. 16 imageBROKER/Alamy Stock Photo; p. 18 Monkey Business Images/Shutterstock.com; p. 19 zixia/Alamy Stock Photo; p. 20 Jerónimo Alba/Alamy Stock Photo; p. 22 Basque Country Mark Baynes /Alamy Stock Photo; p. 24 Migel/Shutterstock.com; p. 26 Christian Bertrand/Shutterstock.com; p. 27 Axel Alvarez/Shutterstock.com; p. 28 Javier Larrea/AGE Fotostock; p. 29 Africa Studio/Shutterstock.com.

Printed in the United States of America

Contents

Introduction 4

Chapter 1 Geography 6

Chapter 2 History 8

Chapter 3 Government 10

Chapter 4 The Economy 12

Chapter 5 The Environment 14

Chapter 6 The People Today 16

Chapter 7 Lifestyle 18

Chapter 8 Religion 20

Chapter 9 Language 22

Chapter 10 Arts and Festivals 24

Chapter 11 Fun and Play 26

Chapter 12 Food 28

Glossary 30

Find Out More 31

Index and About the Author 32

Introduction

Spain is a country in southwestern Europe. It is located on a piece of land called the Iberian **Peninsula**. Spain shares the Iberian Peninsula with a smaller country named Portugal. Spain is the third-largest country in Europe.

There are many different landforms in Spain. The country includes hills, tall mountains, and flat plains. Some parts of Spain have very hot weather. Other parts are cooler.

More than forty million people live in Spain. Most of the people speak Spanish. There are several different **ethnic** and religious groups in Spain. Most Spanish people live in big cities, like the capital city of Madrid. Other people live in the country.

People in Spain enjoy many different sports and pastimes. They enjoy different kinds of food. They celebrate festivals and holidays. Spain has seen some hard times and some wars. However, most of the time, Spain is a peaceful and beautiful place.

Traffic fills the downtown streets of Spain's capital, Madrid.

Spain covers 195,124 square miles (505,370 square kilometers). It is surrounded by three countries: Portugal, France, and Andorra. Spain also borders the Atlantic Ocean and the Mediterranean Sea.

Most of Spain is made up of a high plateau called the Meseta. There

Spain takes up most of the Iberian Peninsula.

are also lowlands along the coast. Spain is very hot in the summer and cold in the winter.

FACT!

The Canary Islands and the Balearic Islands are also part of Spain.

Spain has several mountain ranges. The most important mountain ranges are the Pyrenees and the Cantabrian. Thick forests grow along the sides of these mountains.

A wide sky stretches over Spain's Meseta, an area of flat land and dry heat.

Spain also has many sunny beaches. The country's two major rivers are the Tagus and the Ebro. The Strait of Gibraltar is a narrow body of water. It separates Spain from Africa.

A Long River

The Tagus River is the longest river on the Iberian Peninsula. It flows for 585 miles (940 kilometers) through Spain and Portugal.

People have lived in Spain for more than 100,000 years. One of the earliest groups we know about were the Iberians. Later, other groups came to Spain from different parts of the world.

King Ferdinand and Queen Isabella, two of Spain's most powerful rulers

Spain's empire included large parts of South America, North America, and many islands in the Pacific Ocean.

In the 1400s and 1500s, Spain was a rich and important country. Its kings and queens were some of the most powerful rulers in the world. They sent explorers to other countries and claimed land there.

During the 1600s, Spain lost some of its power. It fought in several wars. Between 1936 and 1939, the Spanish Civil War tore Spain apart. After the war, Spain was ruled by a **dictator**. Then, in 1975, Spain became a **constitutional monarchy**.

A Strong Ruler

Francisco Franco ruled Spain between 1939 and 1975. Franco had complete control over everything in the country.

Generalissimo Francisco Franco

In 1978, Spain approved a new **constitution**. The constitution sets out the laws that the government has to follow. It also said everyone in Spain was equal and had many freedoms.

King Juan Carlos speaks to Parliament in 2011.

Spain's king is a head of the government. However, the king is a symbol. He has no real power. The prime minister is the real head of the government. He or she has a **cabinet**. These officials advise the prime minister.

The constitution divides Spain into seventeen communities. Each community has a government that makes laws for that community.

The government also includes two groups, or houses, of Parliament. Members of Parliament are elected by the people. They make laws. The Supreme Court is a group of judges. They make sure all of Spain's laws are fair.

Capital City

Madrid is the capital of Spain. It is also the largest city. More than three million people live and work there.

Madrid's City Hall, built in the early 1900s

Most people in Spain work in service industries. These industries include tourism, banking, restaurants, stores, and hotels. Many tourists visit Spain's beaches and islands.

Spain is known for its beautiful beaches.

Others visit the country's beautiful mountains or enjoy its city life. Tourism brings in billions of dollars every year.

Many people also work in factories or in industry. Spain's factories make many beautiful clothes. Spain also produces iron and steel to build ships and cars. Spain's mines produce iron, coal, and copper.

FACT!

More than sixty-five million tourists visit Spain each year.

Most people in Spain work in cities. However, farming is also important. Spain's most important crops are cereals, olives, oranges, grapes, and cotton. Some farmers raise cattle, sheep, and pigs.

Money Matters

Spain's money is the euro. Euro coins have different pictures on them. Some coins have pictures of famous places. Others show famous people, such as authors or kings.

Spain is home to many different animals and plants. Rabbits, birds, and foxes live in the grasslands. Eagles, vultures, and a type of goat called a chamois live on rocky cliffs and mountains. Colorful songbirds are found in gardens and woods.

A flock of flamingoes stands in a lagoon in Andalusia, Spain.

Spain's rivers and **wetlands** are full of water birds, mammals, fish, and reptiles. Fish and other sea creatures fill the Mediterranean Sea and the Atlantic Ocean.

The Iberian lynx is one of the rarest mammals in Spain. Fewer than three hundred live in the wild.

Over the years, many animals have become endangered, or risk dying out. As people build more houses, they destroy land. Pollution is also a big problem. Spain is working hard to protect its wetlands and other natural places.

Save the Forests!

Spain's forests have been destroyed by fires or have been cut down to clear land. The government is planting more trees to save Spain's forests.

Many trees in a forest in Galicia have been cut down.

15

More than forty-six million people live in Spain. Some are descended from the original Spanish settlers. Others are descended from different ethnic groups. Basques live in part of northern Spain.

Flamenco dancers wear traditional costumes.

Many Roma people have settled in Spain. Roma are also called gypsies. They travel from place to place. Most of Spain's cities have large Roma populations.

Over the years, people have come to Spain from many different countries. Because Spain is close to northern Africa, many immigrants have moved to Spain from that area. Others came from North Africa, South America, Latin America, and Asia. Most recently, immigrants have come from Middle Eastern countries such as Syria.

FACT!

Many Chinese people immigrated to Spain during the 1920s.

A Unique Culture

Basques have their own language, traditions, sports, and music. Basques have many festivals, called fiestas. These fiestas feature traditional Basque skills such as sheepdog herding, log cutting, and traditional dances.

Lifestyle

People in Spain enjoy spending time with family and friends. They like to share long meals together. Spanish people believe in a relaxed life. They may go to work or school

A Spanish family enjoys a meal together.

until the middle of the afternoon. After lunch, they often take a long nap called a siesta.

Most Spanish people live in cities. They drive cars or take buses and trains to get around. Many city dwellers live in tall apartment buildings. Others live in houses outside the city. People who live in the country might live on a farm.

FACT!

The University of Salamanca was founded in 1218. It is one of the oldest universities in Europe.

By law, women and men have the same rights in Spain. Women go to school and work in many different jobs.

Going to School

Spanish children go to school from ages six to sixteen. Many students go on to university so they can get better jobs.

Many Spanish teenagers spend most of their days in class.

Religion

Most people in Spain are members of the Roman Catholic religion. In the past, the Roman Catholic Church had a lot of power. Everyone had to follow that religion. In 1978, Spain wrote

Most people in Spain are Catholic.

a new constitution. The constitution said that people could follow any religion they wanted. Today, Roman Catholics make up 94 percent of the population.

FACT!

Many Spanish children attend Catholic schools.

Because so many people in Spain are Catholic, religious holidays are celebrated throughout the country. Christmas, Easter, and Three Kings Day are some of the most important holidays.

Spain also has small populations that follow other religions. These religions include Judaism and Islam. Most people who follow these religions live in large cities where they can worship with others of the same faith.

Holy Week

Roman Catholics celebrate Holy Week during the seven days before Easter. Throughout this time, many cities and villages have parades to honor the holiday.

Language

Almost everyone in Spain speaks Spanish. Castilian Spanish is the official language and the one most people speak. It is taught in schools and used at home and at work. It is also spoken by announcers on television and radio.

Students gather in a classroom during a Spanish class.

Language Times Two

In Barcelona, many people speak both Castilian Spanish and Catalan. Road signs are printed in both languages.

FACT!

Most people in Spain can speak at least two languages.

Not everyone speaks Castilian Spanish. People who live in Catalonia also speak Catalan. Catalan Spanish is different from Castilian Spanish. So is Galician Spanish, which is spoken in part of western Spain.

The Basques also have their own language, called Euskara. Euskara is different from any other language spoken in Europe.

Students can learn other languages besides Spanish. Many people learn English or French in school. Immigrants also speak their native languages.

23

Spanish people enjoy the arts, such as theater, art, and music. Traditional Spanish music is very lively. It includes guitars, drums, castanets, and other instruments.

The Festival of San Fermín, or the Running of the Bulls, is held every July in Pamplona, Spain.

Dance is also very popular in Spain. Traditional Spanish dances include the flamenco, the fandango, and the paso doble.

FACT!

The Prado in Madrid is one of the most famous art museums in the world.

What a Mess!

La Tomatina is held in the town Buñol every August. During this festival, people celebrate with a huge, messy tomato fight!

There are many festivals throughout Spain. One of the most famous is the Running of the Bulls. This is held during the Festival of San Fermín. Every year from July 7 to July 14, bulls run through the streets of Pamplona, Spain. Thousands of people come to see the bulls and even run with them.

In Valencia, people celebrate Las Fallas to honor Saint Joseph. Many other festivals have religious themes.

Spain usually has beautiful weather, and Spanish people love to be outside! People take walks and go hiking. Those who live near the coast often enjoy a day at the beach. Swimming and fishing are popular ways to have fun.

RCD Espanyol and Atlético de Madrid play a match in 2016. Soccer is by far the most popular sport in Spain.

Sports are a big part of Spanish life. Soccer, or *fútbol*, is the most popular sport. Each city has its own team and thousands of fans go to their games. People also play soccer in parks and other places just for fun.

FACT!

Basques enjoy a sport called *pelota*. Pelota is a very fast game that is a lot like tennis.

Motor sports are also very popular. Many Formula One racing drivers have come from Spain. Basketball, tennis, and handball are also exciting sports.

Bullfighting

Bullfighting is a traditional Spanish sport. A bullfighter, called a matador, tries to avoid a bull in a large ring. Many people enjoy bullfighting. Other people think the sport is cruel.

A bullfighter, or torero, dazzles a bull in the ring.

Food

Spanish people enjoy many delicious foods. One popular food is a spicy pork sausage called chorizo. Another popular dish is a cold tomato soup called gazpacho.

Friends enjoy a meal at a restaurant serving small dishes of food, called tapas.

Paella is a tasty dish filled with rice, meat, vegetables, and spices.

FACT!

Paella includes different foods in different places. Some areas use fish or shrimp. Other places use beef, chicken, or pork.

Lunch is the big meal of the day in Spain. It can include an appetizer, soup or salad, a main course, and dessert. People drink coffee, hot chocolate, and wine.

Spanish people like sweet desserts, such as churros. Churros are long sticks of fried dough that are covered in sugar and dipped in chocolate.

Delicious Fish

Fish is a favorite food in the Basque region of Spain. People along the coast eat a lot of fish, too. Fish can be eaten whole or chopped up in a stew. Many people enjoy sardines and anchovies served in olive oil.

Seafood paella

Glossary

cabinet A group of advisors to the leader of a country.

constitution A document that describes the laws of a country.

constitutional monarchy A form of government where the king or queen only has limited powers granted by the constitution.

dictator A ruler who has complete control.

ethnic Related to people who have a common national or cultural tradition.

peninsula Land that is surrounded by water on three sides.

wetlands Land that is wet all of the time, such as swamps or bogs.

Find Out More

Books

Guillain, Charlotte. *Spain*. Chicago, IL: Heinemann
    Library, 2012.

Tieck, Sarah. *Spain*. Minneapolis, MN: ABDO
    Publishing Company, 2014.

Website

National Geographic Kids: Spain

http://kids.nationalgeographic.com/explore/

countries/spain/#spain-cliffs.jpg

Video

Spain: Fun Fact Series

https://www.youtube.com/watch?v=0dlDdCUHcDs

This short video includes many interesting facts

about Spain and its people.

Index

cabinet, 10

Catholic, 20–21

cities, 4, 13, 16, 18, 21

constitution, 10–11, 20

constitutional monarchy, 9

dictator, 9

ethnic, 4, 16

king, 8, 10, 13

language, 17, 22–23

peninsula, 4, 6–7

wetlands, 14–15

About the Author

Joanne Mattern is the author of more than 250 books for children. She specializes in writing nonfiction and has explored many different places in her writing. Her favorite topics include history, travel, sports, biography, and animals. Mattern lives in New York State with her husband, four children, and several pets.